P·I·C·T·U·R·E·P·E·D·I·A

NOTE TO PARENTS

This book is part of PICTUREPEDIA, a completely
new kind of information series for children.
Its unique combination of pictures and words
encourages children to use their eyes to discover and
explore the world, while introducing them to a wealth
of basic knowledge. Clear, straightforward text
explains each picture thoroughly and provides
additional information about the topic.

"Looking it up" becomes an easy task with
PICTUREPEDIA, an ideal first reference for all types of
schoolwork. Because PICTUREPEDIA is also entertaining,
children will enjoy reading its words and looking
at its pictures over and over again. You can encourage
and stimulate further inquiry by helping your child
pose simple questions for the whole family to
"look up" and answer together.

PEOPLE
IN THE
PAST

DK

A DK PUBLISHING BOOK

Consultant Margaret Mulvihill

Editor Roz Fishel
Art Editor Ross George

U.S. Editor B. Alison Weir

Series Editor Sarah Phillips
Series Art Editor Paul Wilkinson

Picture Researchers Paul Snelgrove,
Veneta Bullen

Production Manager Ian Paton

Editorial Director Jonathan Reed
Design Director Ed Day

First American edition, 1993
6 8 10 9 7 5

Published in the United States by
DK Publishing, Inc., 95 Madison Avenue
New York, New York 10016

Library of Congress Cataloging-in-Publication Data

People in the past / [Margaret Mulvihill, editor]. — 1st American ed.
    p. cm. — (Picturepedia)
    Includes index.
    Summary: Brief text and illustrations introduce people, events,
customs, and civilizations of the past.
    ISBN 1-56458-217-5
    1. World history—Juvenile literature. 2. World history—
Pictorial works—Juvenile literature. [1. World history.]
    I. Mulvihill, Margaret. II. Series.
D21.P438 1993
909—dc20   92-54483
                                                           CIP
                                                           AC

Reproduced by Colourscan, Singapore
Printed and bound in Italy by Graphicom

PEOPLE
IN THE
PAST

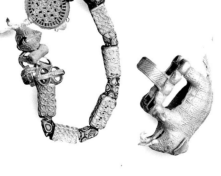

CONTENTS

HUNTERS AND GATHERERS

Horse

The earliest people lived by hunting and gathering to find their food – meat, fish, vegetables, and fruit. They moved with the seasons, sheltering in caves or tents. The animals they hunted gave them food to eat, fat to fuel lamps, skins to make tents and clothes, and bones to make weapons, tent supports, jewelry, and playthings.

Some European hunter-gatherers, who lived 16,000 years ago, painted animal pictures in caves. We don't know exactly why they did this, but cave painting may have been part of their religion or a kind of magic.

Making Flint Tools

Flint is a stone that is easy to work and can be given a sharp edge. The hunter-gatherers used it to make tools and weapons. A pebble or bone hammer was used to strike long flakes of flint from the main stone. The flakes were shaped and then the edges were chipped to make them razor sharp.

The mammoth was like a modern-day elephant, but covered in fur. It was hunted for its meat, skin, and tusks.

An ax with a flint blade

A spear with a bone tip

Animal Magic

Beautiful pictures of the animals hunted by these people were painted on the walls and ceilings of caves in southwest France and in parts of northern Spain.

Bison

Reindeer

The hunters hurled heavy stones at their prey.

The spears used for hunting were often made from a flint or bone arrowhead tied onto a wooden shaft.

The hunters wore clothes made from animal skins.

Unusual Decoration

Teeth and bones from animals were made into pieces of jewelry, such as this necklace.

First Fashion

Animal skins were used to make clothes. First the skins were stretched out, held in place with pegs, and then scraped to clean them and make them soft. Next, the skins were cut to shape. The pieces were sewn together using needles made from animal bone and long, thin strips of hide.

A thong made from animal hide

Skin scrapers

A knife used to cut animal hide

THE EARLY FARMERS

About 12,000 years ago, there was an important change in the way people lived. They began to settle in one place and to farm the land. This happened in the Zagros Mountains in present-day Iran. Here the people discovered how to grow crops for food, and how to tame wild animals to give them meat and milk and to carry heavy loads.

Because the people no longer moved about, they built houses to live in. They learned to spin and weave cloth and also to make pottery.

Bullock

Goat

Sheep

Taming Animals
Young wild animals were caught by hunters and raised on the farms. They provided meat, milk, and wool and were used to carry heavy weights.

Bringing in the Harvest
When the crop was ripe, it was cut down with a sickle. This was made of a sharp flint blade set in a wooden handle.

First Crops
This is emmer wheat. Emmer was developed from the seeds of wild grasses to become an important food source.

A child plays with a stalk of wheat before it is threshed.

Coiling Clay

This girl is making a pot by coiling long, thin rolls of clay on top of a flat clay base. She is making the pot in the same way the first potters did, 9,000 years ago.

The flour would be mixed with water and made into round, flat loaves.

The grain was ground between two heavy stones and made into flour.

From Farm to Town

Farms attracted people. As they grew larger, villages and towns were formed. The first known town, Çatal Hüyük, was built in Turkey about 9,000 years ago.

The walls of the houses were made of mud. Because of this, the houses were not very strong and could only have a few windows.

The roofs were made of branches, reeds, and straw covered in mud.

The houses touched each other, and there were no streets.

People got into their houses by climbing a ladder and going through a hole in the roof.

THE GREAT INVENTORS

A merchant makes a record of the goods he has sold.

About 7,000 years ago, farmers began to move into an area of land between the Tigris and Euphrates rivers. This land was called Mesopotamia, in what is now Iraq. In the south of Mesopotamia was the land of Sumer. The Sumerians were very inventive. They developed the first form of writing and recording numbers and invented the wheel and the plow.

The Sumerians grew bumper crops of cereals, which they traded for things they needed: wood, building stone, or metals. Wheeled carts and their skills in writing and using numbers helped them develop long-distance trade.

How Writing Began

The Sumerians drew pictures on soft clay with a pointed reed. The pictures were drawn downward in lines, from the right-hand side.

Later, they started to write across the tablet, from left to right. The reed tip became wedge shaped, as did the marks it made.

Fish

Bird

Barley

Ox

The signs were then joined together to build up words and sentences.

In time, the picture signs changed so much that the original objects were hard to recognize. This writing is called cuneiform, which means "wedge shaped."

It's a Deal

Instead of writing their names, the Sumerian traders used a seal to sign their contracts.

Flooded Fields

Mesopotamia was watered by the Tigris and the Euphrates, which flooded in the spring. The farmers dug out basins and canals so the river water could be stored and used to water fields away from the river. Because of this, the land was fertile and harvests were good.

Wood was imported from Syria and Lebanon.

Wheeled carts were able to carry heavy objects over long distances.

Pots were used to store grain and oil.

Tilling the Soil

The first plows were made of wood. Later, the blade was made of bronze. Despite the flooding from the rivers, Sumer was baked hard in hot weather. The plow made it possible to break up the hard-to-work soil.

Crosspiece

Spokes

  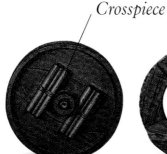 

Revolutionary Invention

The first wheels were made of planks of solid wood held together with crosspieces.

They were clumsy and heavy. In time, lighter wheels were made. These had many spokes.

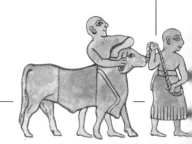

THE EGYPTIANS

The Egyptians believed that when they died, they went on to another, everlasting life. To live happily in the afterlife, they needed their earthly bodies, and great care was taken to ensure that they arrived in style. The dead bodies were preserved in a special way, called mummification.

To mummify a body took a long time, as much as 70 days. First, parts of the body were taken out and put in tightly sealed jars. Next, the body was dried out by covering it with natron, a white powder like salt. It was left for 40 days, rubbed with sweet-smelling oils, and then covered in molten resin. Finally, the body was wrapped in linen to make a neat package.

A picture of the dead person is painted on the mummy case or coffin.

On this coffin, the arms are shown crossed over the chest.

The coffin is made to follow the shape of the body inside.

These little drawings are called hieroglyphs. Each picture means a word or sign in the ancient Egyptian language.

Royal Tombs
Egyptian kings, called pharaohs, were buried in tombs known as pyramids.

Creatures Great and Small

The Egyptians believed in many different gods and goddesses, some of which took the form of animals. They mummified these creatures, as well as people. When treated, they made some odd shapes.

Mummified crocodile

Mummified cow

This coffin is made of wood. Early ones were made of clay or woven out of reeds like a basket.

Mummified cat

\ *Red straps painted on the coffin show that the mummy was a priestess.*

The lid of the coffin is decorated with symbols of the gods. These are the wings of the sky goddess, Nut.

The hieroglyphs may have been spells to help the priestess on her journey to the next life.

Brightly colored figures and symbols are painted on the inside of the coffin.

This mummy case may have been one of a nest of coffins, each fitting inside the next like a set of Russian dolls.

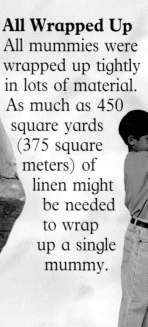

All Wrapped Up
All mummies were wrapped up tightly in lots of material. As much as 450 square yards (375 square meters) of linen might be needed to wrap up a single mummy.

THE WILL TO WIN

All over ancient Greece, festivals were held in honor of the Greek gods. They included competitions in sports, music, and drama. The most famous of the festivals was the Olympic Games, an event first held in 776 BC. There were no team races, and the male athletes competed as individuals. Their prize was a simple wreath of olive leaves, but if you won, you became a hero.

The discus was made of stone or bronze.

The athletes competed barefoot and wore no clothes.

Liftoff!
The long jump was the only jumping event included in Greek athletics.

Fighting Fit
Athletics training kept men fit for war. The connection between sports and war is shown in the race-in-armor event.

The Pentathlon

The decoration on this vase shows athletes training for the pentathlon. The contest included wrestling, throwing the javelin and discus, running, and the long jump.

Handing Over

Relay races were included in some festivals, but not the Olympic Games. The runners used a torch as a baton.

The wooden javelin had a metal tip.

Before they exercised, the athletes rubbed olive oil into their skins to protect them from the sun.

Equal Opportunities

Only men and boys were allowed to compete in the Olympic Games, but in Sparta, girls were expected to go through the same tough athletic training as the boys. This little bronze statue of a girl runner from Sparta shows her barefoot and wearing a short tunic.

Inspiration from the Past

The idea for today's Olympics came from the ancient Greek games of more than 2,000 years ago. The interlocking Olympic rings represent the five continents that compete.

ROMAN LIFE

The Romans planned their towns to include magnificent public buildings such as temples, the town hall, baths, and places of entertainment. There were also grand houses for wealthy families. But side by side with these were the tumbledown dwellings where most people lived – overcrowded apartments built over shops and workshops. They had no toilets or kitchens, and the poor cooked outdoors or bought hot food from stalls. Since the Romans lived, traded, and ate in the streets, their towns were noisy places. Traffic was bad, too, with carts and wagons bringing country goods through the busy streets.

In the Kitchen
This scene shows what a typical Roman kitchen was like. You would have found it in the town house or villa of a rich family.

Country Living
Fine houses, called villas, were built on estates in the countryside.

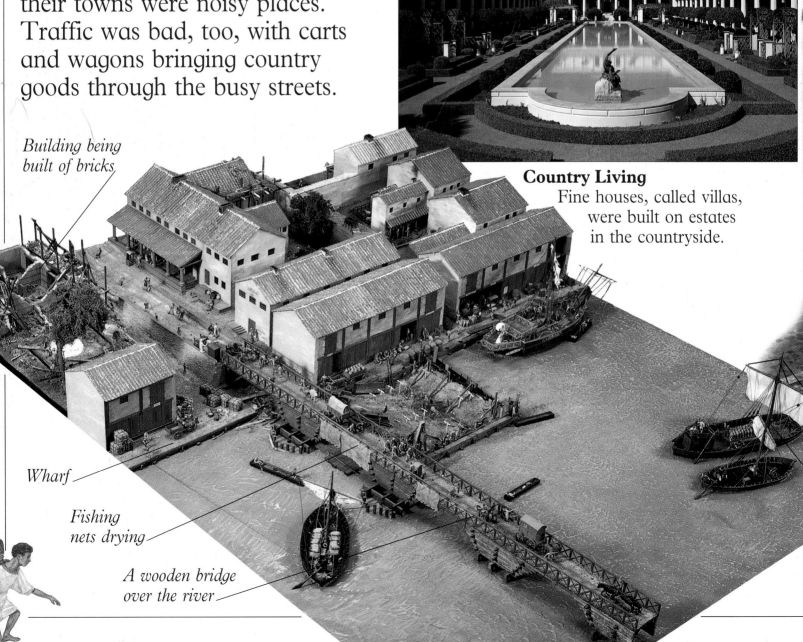

Building being built of bricks

Wharf

Fishing nets drying

A wooden bridge over the river

Herbs dried over the stove. The Romans liked their food highly flavored. Herbs and spices also helped make food keep longer.

Bread was an important part of Roman diet and the basic food of the poor.

Slaves did the housework for wealthy Romans.

A saucepan made of bronze

Jugs for serving wine

Storage jars, called amphorae, were used to hold wine.

A sailing boat carries cargo from the port.

Cats were kept as pets for children and to chase away mice and rats!

The floor was centrally heated. This worked by sending warmed air through pipes laid under the floor.

Modern Conveniences
Unlike the poor in their cramped dwellings, wealthy Romans lived in well-planned houses with lots of home comforts. There was running water, a toilet and bathroom, a kitchen, and even central heating. In many ways, a Roman house was not unlike the one you live in today.

FOOD FROM THE NEW WORLD

Sunflower

Cocoa

From 1492 onward, European explorers sailed across the Atlantic to what they called the New World of North and South America. There they discovered a treasure trove of gold and silver. But they found other treasures, too. These were foods that grew only in the New World, such as maize and potatoes, and plants that could be made into medicines.

In fact, you may be surprised to find out how many of the foods you eat come from the Americas. Every time you eat a tomato or some mashed potato or have chocolate for a treat, just think: you owe them to the people of North and South America.

A World of Golden Treasure
The Indian peoples of America had vast quantities of gold, which they used to make into jewelry. The Europeans plundered most of this treasure.

Maize was eaten boiled, roasted, or ground into flour. The explorer Christopher Columbus took it back to Europe when he returned from his voyages.

This is corn meal, made out of ground corn. It was used to make breadlike foods.

Peanut

Native American Plants
These include cocoa (for chocolate), sunflowers (for cooking oil), and peanuts.

"Pyne fruit," or pineapple, was one of the new fruits found by the explorers. Pineapples were also used to make wine.

Black beans

Healing Plants
When the explorers reached the Americas, they found skilled healers among the people living there. These healers used thousands of plants to make medicines. Their remedies were used to cure many illnesses, including stomach pains, headaches, coughs, and fevers. Many of these plants are still used today to make medicines.

Cinchona leaf

Quinine is used to prevent an illness called malaria. It is made from the bark of the cinchona tree.

Cinchona bark

Quinine tablets

Lots of different beans came from Mexico. These are red beans.

These small, hot peppers are chilies. They were used to flavor the bowls of maize porridge that the Mexicans ate for breakfast.

Sweet potatoes

Tomatoes started off as weeds growing in the maize fields. In time, different kinds were grown to eat. The first ones to reach Europe were probably yellow.

Potatoes were first grown in the Andes Mountains. They were loaded aboard the treasure ships as food for the sailors.

Avocados look like pears with rough, tough skins. They were first grown in Central America.

RAIDERS FROM THE SEA

Late in the eighth century, a seafaring people from the countries now known as Denmark, Norway, and Sweden began to sail abroad in search of new homelands. They were called Vikings. In their amazingly fast and adaptable longships, Vikings were the best sailors in Europe. They often behaved like pirates. Then, gradually, the Vikings began to settle in the lands they had once raided, although they continued to be great sea traders. Many of the Vikings became Christians. It was the Vikings who founded the cities of Dublin in Ireland and Kiev in the Ukraine. The Normans were descended from Viking settlers in northern France.

The mast supported a big square sail. This was used when the longship was out at sea and there was plenty of wind to fill the sail.

Longships were called "serpents of the sea." They were fitted with fearsome animal carvings, called prowheads.

As Vikings prepare to land on a foreign shore, warriors stand at the front of the longship, with settlers in the middle.

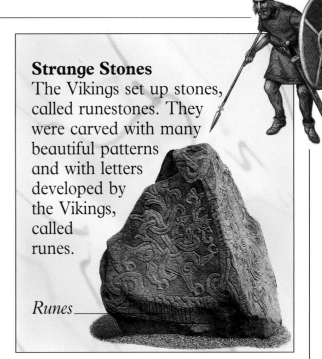

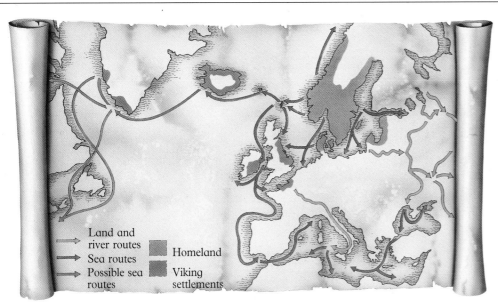

Strange Stones

The Vikings set up stones, called runestones. They were carved with many beautiful patterns and with letters developed by the Vikings, called runes.

Runes

Where the Vikings Went

The Vikings roamed great distances. Merchants traveled to Russia, Iran, and around the Mediterranean Sea. They traded such northern things as furs and walrus tusks for southern things, such as silk and silver. Explorers sailed to Europe, Iceland, Greenland, and also Newfoundland in North America. They called this Vinland.

Fascinating Tales

Storytelling was very popular. These stories, or sagas, were long poems telling of brave deeds, journeys to strange lands, and victories in battle. When people couldn't read or write, they remembered stories by learning them by heart.

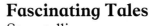

Longships were made of overlapping planks of wood. They were very light and could be carried overland for short distances to get from one river to another.

THE CRUSADES

The city of Jerusalem and the Holy Land of Palestine (now Israel and Jordan) are special to people of three faiths – Jews, Muslims, and Christians. About 900 years ago, several wars were fought in the Middle East for control of Jerusalem. Muslims seized the city and refused to allow in Christians. As a result, European Christians – called crusaders from the Spanish word *cruzada*, meaning "marked with a cross" – set out to take Jerusalem.

After four years of struggle, the crusaders captured Jerusalem in 1099 and held it for nearly 100 years. Then it was recaptured by a great Muslim leader called Saladin. More crusades followed, but none was successful. However, the returning crusaders brought many new objects and ideas back to Europe.

This crusader knight is wearing armor called chain mail.

Over his armor, the knight is wearing a loose white coat with a cross on it – the sign of a crusader.

The leg pieces are made of chain mail.

Stronghold
The crusaders built strong castles in the Arab style to defend the land they had captured. This is Krak des Chevaliers in Syria.

Body Beautiful

The crusaders took back to Europe new customs that they learned in the Middle East. Cosmetics such as rouge to redden the cheeks and henna to color hair became common for women. Glass mirrors replaced polished metal discs. Perfumes to scent clothes and the body were used. Being clean became popular!

This puppet of a Muslim Arab is fighting a Christian knight. For centuries, puppets have been used to act out folktales, religious stories, and famous battles and scenes from history.

A Muslim foot soldier usually carried a round shield for protection. It may have been made of wood or of layers of hardened leather sewn together.

Boots made of leather or felt were the most common footwear for a Muslim soldier.

Roman numerals

I   II   III   IV   V   VI   VII   VIII   IX

Arabic numerals

0 1 2 3 4 5 6 7 8 9

One, Two, Three . . .

The Muslims developed a series of numbers, called Arabic numerals, that were much easier to use than those of the old Roman system. They are used today throughout the world.

Bookworms

Arab learning was more advanced than that of the crusaders. They had lots of books and libraries at a time when there were very few in Europe. The crusaders took many books back with them.

Healing Arts

Muslim doctors were very good surgeons and were skilled in using plants and herbs to make medicines. They used opium and myrrh to ease pain when people were having operations.

Musical Instruments

The Muslims invented a musical instrument called the al'ud, which was called the lute in Europe. The modern guitar was developed from this instrument.

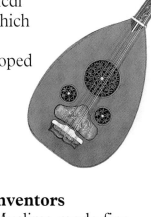

Great Inventors

The Muslims made fine scientific instruments to increase their knowledge of the world. They used astrolabes to help them find their way when traveling through empty deserts.

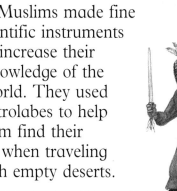

MARCO POLO

In 1271, a merchant called Marco Polo and his family set off from Venice on an extraordinary journey to China. They traveled along the Silk Road, an important trading route between Europe and the Far East. Merchants had been using the route for over 1,700 years before the Polos, but they were the first to travel its whole length. In an age when there were no planes, trains, buses, or cars, they crossed thousands of miles of mountains, deserts, and plains on foot, on horses, and even on camels. Their journey to China took them over three years. The Silk Road could be very dangerous, and the traders were sometimes attacked by bandits. Because of this threat, they traveled together in groups.

Making a Swap
The Venetian merchants exchanged jewels, silver, and gold for goods from the East that were highly valued in Europe. These included spices, silks, porcelain or "China," and fine carpets.

Wealthy Traders
Venice was the most important port in Europe. Its merchants traveled by sea and land to bring back goods from the East to sell to other towns in Europe.

Camels were used by merchants when crossing the desert regions of central Asia. Unlike horses, they were able to travel long distances without needing water.

Besides the barren deserts, the merchants traveling on the Silk Road had to climb over fearsome mountain ranges and cross flooded rivers.

Pepper

Cloves

Cinnamon

Mace   Nutmeg

Silk tunic

In the desert, travelers had to take all their own food and water with them.

A camel train was part of a caravan, a large group of people who traveled together.

Persian carpet

Porcelain jar

The camel driver is covered from head to foot in heavy clothing to protect him from the harsh winds of the desert.

In the Court of Kublai Khan
When the Polos arrived in China, they found it under the control of the Mongol emperor Kublai Khan. Marco Polo stayed at the Mongol court for 17 years and became a trusted advisor to Kublai Khan.

THE RENAISSANCE

In the 15th century, Europe was bursting with new ideas about art, learning, and religion. Many of the people who could read and write began to ask questions and to do experiments for themselves rather than follow what their rulers and priests told them to think. They rediscovered many of the ideas that the Greeks and Romans had about life and the world. As a result, this period became known as the "Renaissance," a French word meaning "rebirth." The Renaissance started in the cities of northern and central Italy but gradually spread all over Europe.

Renaissance artists used live models and made them look real in their paintings.

A letter of type used in the printing press

The Printed Word
Before the printing press was invented by Johannes Gutenberg, books had to be copied by hand. Only the rich could afford them.

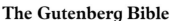

Everyday objects were used as props in the paintings.

The apprentice is grinding colors to make paints for his master. He will mix the powder with oil to produce oil paints.

The Gutenberg Bible
These pages come from one of the three books that made up the Gutenberg Bible. It was printed in the 1450s and was much admired for its quality.

In the 15th century, artists began to paint on canvas using oil paints. Before then, they had mainly used water-based paints.

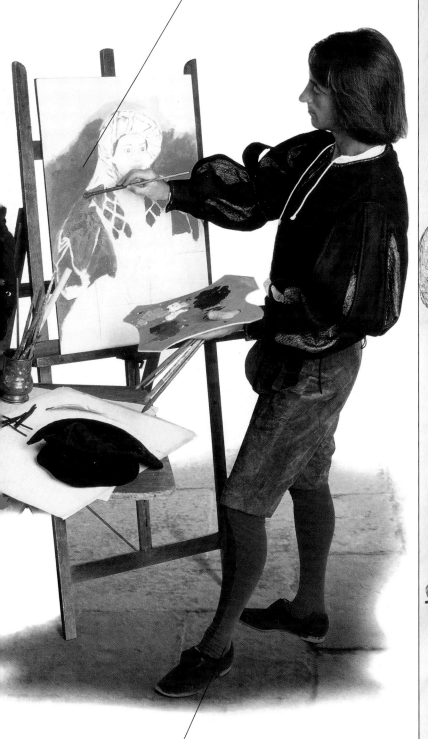

Artists were no longer unknown craftsmen, and their names became famous throughout Europe during the Renaissance.

The Quest for Knowledge
During the Renaissance, scholars and scientists began doing experiments and inventing things to find out more about the world they lived in.

With the invention of the telescope, faraway planets could be seen in detail for the first time.

The artist Leonardo da Vinci was interested in the workings of the human body. This is one of his drawings.

This model was made from a design by Leonardo, showing an early kind of tank.

Leonardo's creative imagination led him to produce designs for a flying machine.

THE WAY OF THE WARRIOR

For about 700 years, the Samurai were the honored knights of Japan. Fierce fighters, they had a tough training, becoming experts in fencing, wrestling, archery, and acrobatics, and they had a special code of behavior. The word "samurai" means "one who serves," and any Samurai worthy of the name was absolutely loyal to his lord, ready to obey any command without question.

But although the Samurai were professional fighters, away from battle they were not violent men. The Samurai believed in Zen Buddhism, a religion that taught respect for all living things. The Samurai were also taught to love art and learning, taking pride in their skill at painting, writing poetry, and even flower arranging.

The large horned helmet was meant to terrify enemies as much as to protect its wearer.

Western Merchants
When the Portuguese arrived in Japan in 1543 they brought guns with them. The guns completely changed warfare in Japan and caused great changes to the way of life.

Women and Ladies

Just as the Samurai obeyed his lord, so the women of his own family had to obey him. Graceful, musical, and artistic, these Samurai ladies were expected to make homes for their lords and masters.

By contrast, the peasant women who labored in the fields had to work as hard as beasts of burden.

A Samurai's most important weapons were his two razor-sharp swords, one long, the other short. At birth, every Samurai boy was presented with a sword, which he kept for life.

A Samurai's armor consisted of six main pieces: the helmet, the face mask, the breastplate, the sleeves, the shin guards, and the loin guard.

Knowing Their Place

Life in Samurai Japan was strictly organized. From birth, everybody had a fixed place in society. Samurai families belonged to the upper classes.

The godlike Emperor was the official ruler, but the Shogun, his chief general, was really the most powerful person in Japan.

Shogun

The Daimyo were the nobles of Japan, and they were supported by Samurai warriors. They preferred to have nothing to do with money or the buying and selling of goods.

Daimyo

Samurai

Merchants and traders were not given much respect, in spite of their wealth.

Merchants

Lowest of the low were the peasants. They worked on the farms of the Daimyo and were treated like slaves.

Peasant

Newcomers to a New Land

The Europeans who began arriving in North America in the beginning of the 17th century were traders and settlers rather than soldier-conquerors. At first, the contact between them and the people already living there, whom they called Indians, was friendly. The Native Americans showed the newcomers how to hunt, fish, and farm in a land of plenty. In return for their help and animal furs, the Native Americans were given objects such as knives, needles, fishhooks, and cloth. But before long, the settlers were taking more and more land for themselves and trying to change the ways of the Indians.

Warm furs from the forest animals of North America were taken back to Europe and sold for high prices.

European weapons, tools, and machines completely changed hunting and warfare for the Indians.

European cloth was prized for its bright colors and silkiness.

Creek
(Southeast)

Iroquois
(Northeast)

Tlingit
(Pacific Northwest)

Hidatsa
(Plains)

Hopi
(Southwest)

*The settlers gave the
Indians silk thread
and glass beads.
The Indians used
feathers and animal
teeth to decorate
themselves.*

Sauk
(Great Lakes)

Paiute
(Great Basin)

Warriors and Hunters

The work that men and women
did varied from tribe to tribe, but
usually the men were the hunters
and warriors, while the women were
the farmers and homemakers. Most
Indians wore their hair long, and
they enjoyed decorating their bodies
and clothes.

Tepees, Longhouses, and Pueblos

There was great variety in the lives
of the Native American peoples.
How they lived – their clothes,
their food, their religious beliefs –
depended on the land and the
weather. Some of the differences
between the tribes are shown
by their homes.

*For comfort
and protection
against ants, snakes,
and other dangers, the
Indians wore slipper-
like leather shoes,
called moccasins.*

*Sweet corn, squash, and
pumpkins were among
the exotic American foods
that the Europeans
tasted for the
first time.*

Tlingit cedar-
plank house

Plains Indian
animal-skin tepee

Sauk mat-covered
dome lodge

Paiute brush
and reed
encampment

Iroquois
wooden
longhouse

Hopi stone
and sun-baked
mud-brick pueblo

Creek
storehouse

KINGDOM OF GOLD

Ghana

The Ashanti kingdom flourished for 200 years after its emergence in the 17th century in what is now Ghana in West Africa. The Ashanti were a highly organized people: the king had his own civil service, which carried out his commands throughout the country. The Ashanti were also fine warriors, and much of their wealth was based on selling slaves from the prisoners they captured in battle. They had vast quantities of gold, which was used to make jewelry and to decorate musical instruments and weapons. Ashanti goldsmiths were highly skilled in their craft. They used a special method to cast the metal, called the lost-wax technique.

The item to be cast in gold was modeled in melted beeswax.

The wax was made into thin sheets. These were cut into strips, which were used to make the model.

Clay was molded around the model, and a hole was made in the clay. As the mold was baked, the wax melted and poured out through the hole. Molten gold was then poured into the space.

When the metal had cooled and hardened, the mold was smashed open. The gold object was taken out and cleaned up.

Beautifully Made
These royal sandals have flowers of gold sewn onto them.

Ashanti goldsmiths worked gold into all kinds of objects. The handle of this sword was covered in a fine sheet of gold.

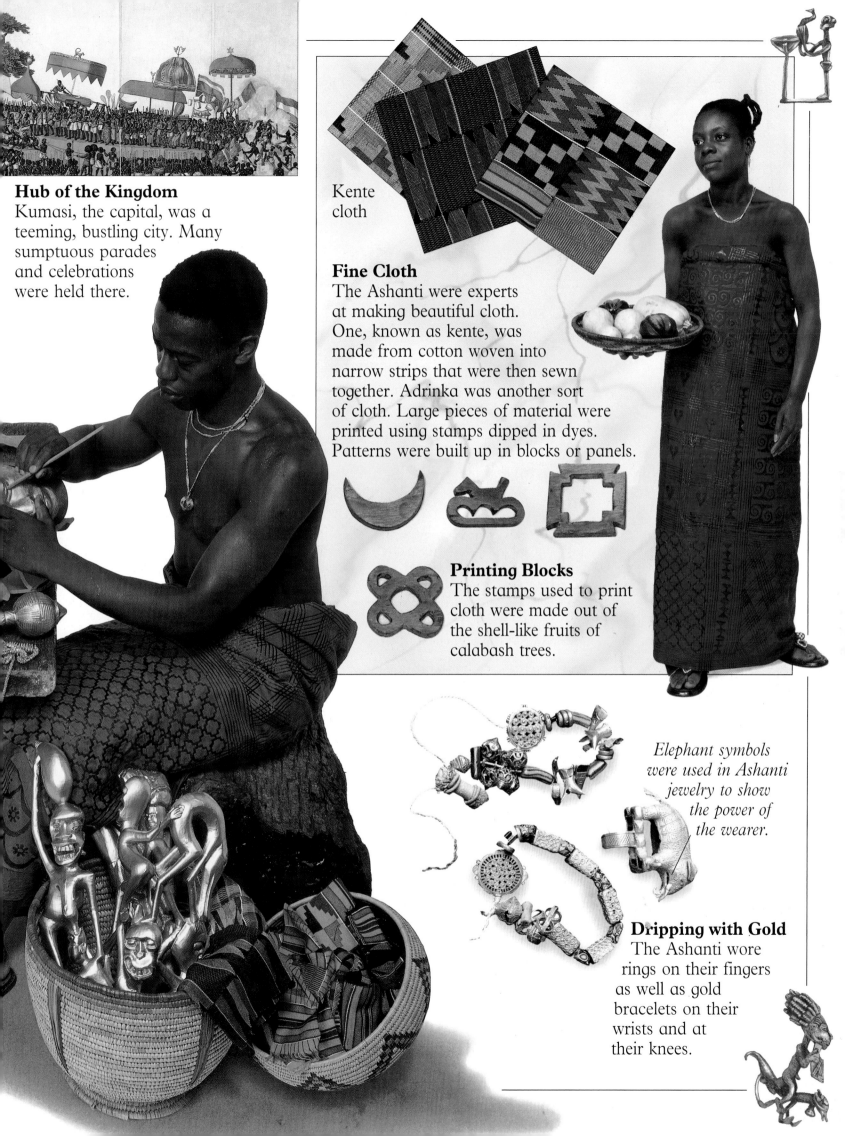

Hub of the Kingdom

Kumasi, the capital, was a teeming, bustling city. Many sumptuous parades and celebrations were held there.

Kente cloth

Fine Cloth

The Ashanti were experts at making beautiful cloth. One, known as kente, was made from cotton woven into narrow strips that were then sewn together. Adrinka was another sort of cloth. Large pieces of material were printed using stamps dipped in dyes. Patterns were built up in blocks or panels.

Printing Blocks

The stamps used to print cloth were made out of the shell-like fruits of calabash trees.

Elephant symbols were used in Ashanti jewelry to show the power of the wearer.

Dripping with Gold

The Ashanti wore rings on their fingers as well as gold bracelets on their wrists and at their knees.

CATHERINE THE GREAT

Catherine II, Empress of Russia during the 18th century, was called "Great" because she worked hard as ruler of her vast empire. She asked the advice of many of the major thinkers in Europe, and because she was interested in education, she started the Russian school system.

Catherine also loved clothes and spectacular entertainments, and so did her nobles. Under her rule, they became even more powerful than they had been before. They were the owners of land and of people. These people were known as serfs and, like slaves, they had to do whatever their masters wanted. Serfs could be bought and sold by their masters.

Miserable Existence
Nine out of ten Russians were serfs, and life for them was grim. Often, they lived in poor log huts with only one room for an entire family.

Catherine's palaces and the homes of the nobles were filled with furniture, ornaments, carpets, and other luxuries in the latest fashions.

The Hermitage

Catherine built a Winter Palace in St. Petersburg. She called it the Hermitage, because it allowed her to shut herself and her court away like hermits. Today it is a famous museum.

During court entertainments, the wearing of masks became popular.

The court entertainments were dazzling to look at, with gorgeous costumes.

The playing of music was encouraged at court. Catherine invited foreign musicians to Russia to perform their work.

The nobles dressed in clothes that came from fashionable France. They were the finest clothes money could buy.

Revolt of the Serfs

In 1771, a Cossack soldier called Emilian Pugachev set himself up as a rival emperor to Catherine. The Cossacks were a warlike people who lived in southern Russia. Thousands of serfs who wanted to get rid of the nobles joined in their revolt.

The number of rebels under Pugachev grew, and in 1773, they swarmed across Russia, destroying the city of Kazan. Catherine ordered her army to attack the rebels, and in July 1774, the serfs were defeated. Pugachev was captured, brought to Moscow, and executed. The revolt was over.

TO THE ENDS OF THE WORLD

In the 18th century, a great explorer called James Cook made three voyages that mapped the Pacific Ocean, the world's largest and deepest sea. On his first voyage, he sailed around New Zealand and down the east coast of Australia. On the second journey, he explored the Antarctic and mapped many South Pacific islands. On his last trip, he discovered Hawaii.

Cook's voyages were important because, unlike many explorers before him, he was not interested in conquest. Instead, he tried to find out about the people, the plants, and the animals of the countries he visited. On board his ship were scientists, artists, and collectors, as well as officers, crew, and servants.

South Sea Paradise
Throughout the 18th century, artists and writers presented life in the South Pacific as being easy and perfect.

Because they were members of the Royal Navy, Cook and his companions wore naval uniforms.

The first voyage to the South Seas was made to watch the movement of the planet Venus. The scientists looked through a telescope like this.

This very accurate astronomical clock was used for timing the observations of the stars and planets.

Art for All

Drawings and paintings made by the artists on Cook's voyages were published. People in Europe could see illustrations of new plants and animals discovered on the explorations.

Erythrina

Hibiscus

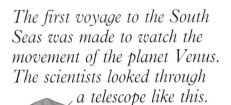

This is a quadrant. It was another means of helping sailors find their way.

Wildcat

Butterfly fish

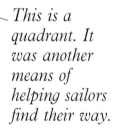

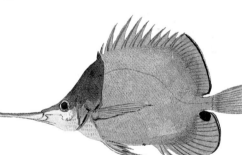

Blue-crowned lory

Artists were taken on the voyages to draw the plants and animals they saw, just as a photographer might take pictures today.

REVOLUTION

The revolutionaries were against organized religion, and many clergymen fled the country.

In the 18th century, an important revolution started in France. It happened because the king, Louis XVI, and his nobles held all the power and wealth in the country. He could rule the people as he pleased. The way he chose to do so was unfair. For example, the nobles, who were already rich, paid no taxes while the poor peasants did.

In 1789, the king had nearly run out of money. He wanted to increase taxes. At the same time, food was very scarce because of bad harvests. The ordinary people had had enough and decided that they didn't want to be ruled by the king. Louis was executed, and a new government was set up.

Nobles were thought to be enemies of the revolution. Some were arrested and went to the guillotine.

The revolution was supported by people who thought they had been badly treated by their rulers. They included lawyers, traders, small farmers, workers, and ordinary soldiers.

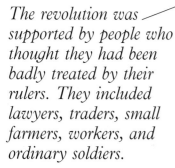

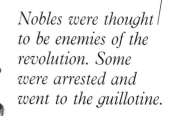

The nobles made fun of the simple clothes of the revolutionaries. They called them sans-culottes, people without the fine knee-length breeches the nobles wore.

Women played an important part in revolutionary events. They led many of the marches.

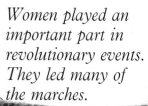

The Guillotine

Anyone who was not loyal to the revolution faced arrest and possible death by guillotine. The guillotine cut off the heads of the victims. It was made of a heavy, sharp blade that fell between two posts. Death by guillotine was very quick. It caused less suffering than other methods of execution.

Victims of the guillotine rode to the place of execution in open carts, called tumbrils.

The revolutionaries wore a red bonnet that looked like a nightcap. It was decorated with a blue and white ribbon.

American Revolution

In the 17th century, people left Europe to live in America. They were ruled from Britain and were called colonists. Eventually, they wanted to rule themselves and fought the British for their independence. The French revolutionaries were encouraged by the American success.

This painting shows colonists fighting the British in Massachusetts in 1775.

RICHES OF INDUSTRY

One of the biggest changes in the history of the world, the Industrial Revolution, started in Britain in the late 18th century. As the "Workshop of the World," Britain was the first home of new machines, new types of materials, and new ways of making power. This was the age of coal and iron, of gas and electricity, of railways and factories.

Within 50 years, this series of mighty inventions had dramatically changed the way in which people lived. Railways and steamships made it possible to travel quickly from place to place. Instead of living in the country, many more people lived in towns and cities. There they worked in factories where machines made things in vast numbers, quickly and cheaply.

The railways and cheaper paper provided many more readers with news of events from all over the world.

Grim Conditions
The big industrial cities were very smoky, and many people were crammed together in badly built houses.

With the arrival of trains, which had to run according to timetables, people began to live their lives by the clock.

Iron Foundry
Abraham Darby replaced charcoal (made from wood) with coke (made from coal) for making a new kind of tough iron.

The invention of electroplating made it possible to coat iron objects with silver. They looked like solid silver but were far cheaper to make.

Vast numbers of machine-made cups and plates were turned out for everyday use.

Made of Metal
Engineers soon made use of iron and steel. In 1789, Abraham Darby III built the first iron bridge across the river Severn. It is now called Ironbridge. The Eiffel Tower was built in France in 1889, and is nearly 330 yards (300 m) high.

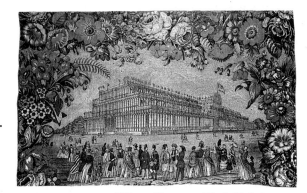

The invention of artificial dyes in the 1850s meant that cloth did not fade when it was washed.

The Great Exhibition
In 1851, the Great Exhibition was opened in London inside a huge glass building called the Crystal Palace. The Exhibition displayed all the latest industrial developments.

Factory Life
The first factories were built to contain the heavy machinery needed to produce cotton cloth. Whole families – even young children – kept the machines going night and day.

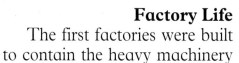

PIONEERS

During the 19th century, European settlers traveled across America in search of land to farm. They were called pioneers. Some of them traveled in wagon trains so long that they stretched as far as the eye could see. The wagons were packed tight with provisions – food, tools, plows, household goods, and even chamber pots. There was room only for small children, the sick, and some women to ride in the wagons. Everyone else walked alongside.

Tormented by the heat and dust or by gales, rain, and snow, the pioneers trudged across prairies and climbed over mountains. They lived and slept outdoors and were often short of food and water. The pioneers also faced attacks from Native Americans, who resented the Europeans' taking their land from them.

The wagons were pulled by teams of horses, mules, or oxen.

The wheels at the front were made smaller than those at the back so that the wagon could be steered more easily.

The Lure of Gold
Prospectors were people who hunted for gold. They would fill a shallow pan with gravel from a riverbed and wash the stones out of the pan with water. Then they looked for any gold that might have sunk to the bottom.

When gold was discovered in Australia, America, South Africa, and Canada in the 19th century, Europeans flocked to these countries to make their fortune.

Self-assembly

When the pioneers came to set up home, they had to build their own houses. Some made them out of logs, but others used chunks of dry earth cut from the ground.

The Great Trek

In 1835, Dutch settlers in South Africa moved in wagons to new land to escape being ruled by the British. This journey was called the Great Trek. For safety against the Africans whose land they had entered, the settlers would carefully form their wagons into a circle at night.

The top was made of canvas held up by a frame of hoops. It helped keep out rain and dust.

The hoops were made of strong and flexible hickory wood.

The pioneers had to bring all their cooking equipment with them.

The wheels were made of wood, and the rim was covered in iron. Wheels often broke and held up the wagon train.

THE AMERICAN CIVIL WAR

In 1861, a civil war started in America between states in the South that allowed slavery and states in the North that did not. The South tried to break away from the Union to form a separate nation, but the North went to war to prevent this. After four years of bitter fighting, the North won, and the South was forced to return to the Union. But the price paid by both sides was terrible. Some 620,000 soldiers died, over half of them victims of disease, not of battle. When they fell ill or were wounded, their treatment was as likely to kill them as cure them. The field hospitals were filthy and the surgeons often poorly trained.

If they were lucky, soldiers were given drugs to make them unconscious during surgery. But often they had nothing to ease the pain.

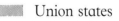

Union states

Confederate states

Border states that fought on the Northern side

Areas with the most slaves

Other territories

The Confederates
The soldiers of the South, or Confederacy, were given uniforms of gray coats and caps and blue trousers. When uniforms were in short supply, the men wore whatever they could find.

The Unionists

The soldiers of the North, or Union, wore dark blue coats or jackets and sky blue trousers. They had more and better weapons than the troops from the South because most of the factories making weapons were in the North.

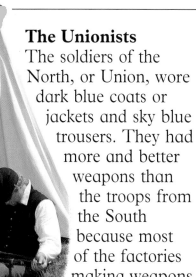

The Slave States

The wealth of the southern states of America came from plantations producing cotton, sugar, and tobacco. The work on the plantations was carried out by slaves – Africans who had been captured and shipped from Africa over to America. Their masters could do what they liked with them, and they were often ill-treated. Slavery was finally ended in America in 1865.

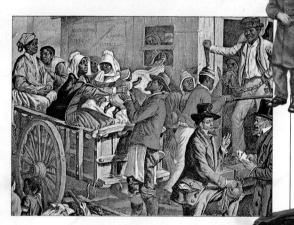

Slaves could be bought and sold in markets like animals. Often families were split up.

The surgeons who treated the soldiers often worked with dirty hands and clothes spattered with blood.

Women volunteered to help the wounded. In the North, teams of trained nurses were set up.

Most medicines were not very effective, and a few were actually dangerous.

Special Kit

With its pliers and saw, this box looks like a tool kit. In fact, it was a surgeon's case used during the American Civil War.

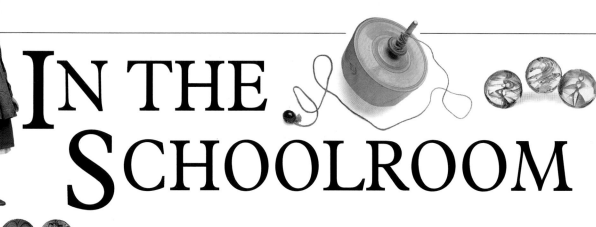

IN THE SCHOOLROOM

The chalkboard was double-sided. It was on wheels so it could be moved easily.

Until 1870, children in England did not have to go to school. Children from rich families went to school, but poor families could not afford to pay for education. Poor children had to go to work to help their parents. After 1870, the government made school places available to young children for a very small payment. By 1902, education was free, and every child aged between 5 and 13 had to attend school.

At school, children were taught reading, writing, arithmetic, and religion. The children sat at their desks, chanting spellings and tables over and over again and copying words onto slates. At other times, they did some geography and history, drawing, singing, and physical exercise. Discipline was very strict, and children were beaten if they made mistakes in their work.

The globe of the world was used to teach geography to the children.

A wooden hoop used for playing

Playtime
When they were not in school, children amused themselves with outdoor games like the ones played today – marbles, skipping, hopscotch, and football. Hoops were popular, too – they were rolled along the ground, thrown in the air, or whirled around the body.

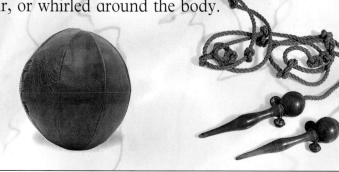

China inkwells in a tray were filled and given out to the older children by a monitor. The children wrote with pen and ink in a special copybook.

The ink to fill the inkwells was kept in a special container that looked like a small watering can.

The window was built high up so that the children could not look out and be distracted from their work.

Teachers often carried a cane with them. If the children were bad, they would be smacked.

This is an abacus, or counting frame. Children learned to add and subtract by moving the beads along the wires.

Each child in the class had only one reading book. It contained stories and poems and had to last the whole year.

Young children did their writing on slates, using slate pencils. The slates were cheap and could be used over and over again.

The desks were very simple. The shelf underneath held the children's books.

Pencils were made of a single piece of lead, without a wooden casing.

The desks had special holes made in them to hold the inkwells.

Stitch by Stitch

Samplers were very popular in schools. They consisted of a piece of embroidery designed to show a girl's skill in using different stitches. Girls began to make them at an early age. They were a way of teaching girls their letters and their sewing at the same time.

GLOSSARY

Chain mail A type of armor made of joined-up metal links or rings.

Christopher Columbus 1451-1506 Italian-born explorer who discovered the Americas in the 15th century.

Cuneiform The wedge-shaped writing invented in the area of Mesopotamia.

Electroplating The covering of one metal with a coating of another, particularly iron with silver.

Guillotine A machine used during the French Revolution to execute people by beheading them.

Hieroglyphs The kind of picture writing used in ancient Egypt.

Industrial Revolution The time about 200 years ago in Europe when machines powered by water and then steam gradually replaced hand- and horse-driven machinery.

Kublai Khan 1216-1294 Mongol conqueror and emperor of China whose court was visited by Marco Polo.

Leonardo da Vinci 1452-1519 Italian painter, sculptor, architect, and engineer.

Longhouse A long house made of wood and bark and lived in by several families of Native Americans.

Longship A narrow, open ship with oars and a square sail, used by the Vikings.

Lost-wax technique Method of making a mold for gold objects using wax surrounded by clay.

Marco Polo 1254-1324 Venetian merchant famous for his travels to Asia.

Mummification In ancient Egypt, the process of preserving a dead body using powder, oils, and resins. The body is then wrapped in linen bandages.

Native Americans The people living in North America before it was conquered by Europeans. The first settlers called them "Indians."

Olympic Games In ancient Greece, a festival of sports held every four years in honor of the gods.

Pioneers Explorers or settlers of a new land.

Prospectors People who search a region looking for gold in rocks and sand.

Prowhead A figure, often an animal, carved in wood and fitted on the front of a ship.

Pueblo A village of joined-up houses made of stone or mud bricks, such as the ones lived in by certain Native Americans.

Renaissance A period when scholars in Europe studied ancient Greece and Rome and developed new ways of thinking about the world around them.

Rune A sign or letter from the Viking alphabet.

Saladin 1138-1193 A great Muslim leader who fought against the Crusaders.

Samurai Japanese warriors, or knights, who followed strict rules of behavior.

Sans-culottes During the French Revolution, the name given to the revolutionaries who were too poor to afford the fine breeches that were worn by gentlemen.

Silk Road A route for traders traveling between Europe and Asia.

Sparta Ancient Greek city and its surrounding region, famous for its strict discipline and tough way of life.

Tepee A tent made of animal skins used by Native Americans.

Tumbril A type of cart that was used to carry condemned prisoners to the guillotine.

Villa In Roman times, a large, fine country house and estate.

Acknowledgments

Photography: Andy Crawford, Steve Gorton, Ray Moller, Tim Ridley, James Stevenson

Illustrations: Ray Hutchins, Chris Lyon, Roger Stewart

Models: Peter Griffiths

Thanks to: Africraft; Alison Verity Civil War Library Museum, Philadelphia, Pennsylvania; Clubb Chipperfield Ltd; English Heritage; Farah Eskafi; Hermitage House, Beaulieu; Historical Newspaper Services; London Museum; Michael Jay, the Soma Horse Association and the Tenshin Shoden Katori Shinto Ryu; Morris Angels and Son Ltd; National Maritime Museum; Scallywags Child Model Agency; Southern Skirmish Association; Weal & Downland Open Air Museum

Index